I am pleasantly
and
comfortably me

Written By Kazia Alysse

Illustrated By QBN Studios

This book is dedicated to all the neurodivergent children out there who are navigating through a world that may not always understand them.

To those who endure sensory overload, social anxiety, and communication challenges, we see you and we celebrate your unique perspectives and strengths. May this book serve as a reminder that you are not alone and your differences are nothing to be ashamed of but rather something to be proud of. May you continue to shine bright and inspire others to embrace their own journeys.

With love and admiration,

Kazia Alysse

I am pleasantly and comfortably me.

I am always filled with happiness and glee.

I love to go to the arcade and play.
"Ping Pong is my favorite," I always say.

I love to go to the beach and play in the water.

I love to see the animals especially the otter.

I love to learn about everything at the zoo.
I like tigers, and bears, and crocodiles too.

I love to eat and I like to cook,
But sometimes I need a recipe book.

I love to make my favorite dish.
I also like to go and fish.

I like to play and sleep with my favorite toys. I take them to the car with the beeping noise.

I love pets so silly and fluffy.

I love every dog no matter how scruffy.

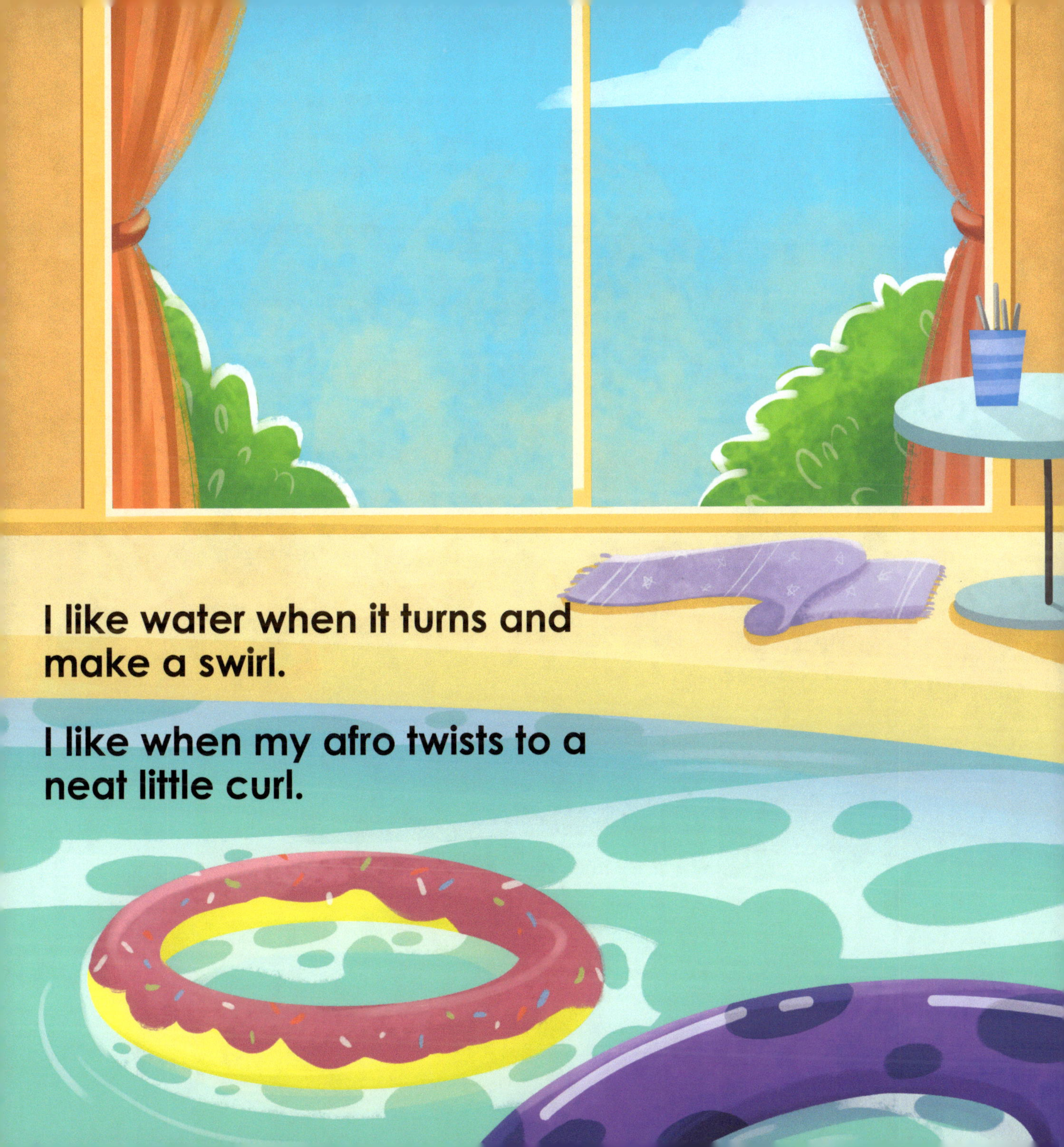

I like water when it turns and make a swirl.

I like when my afro twists to a neat little curl.

I love to pretend and make a big dinosaur roar!

I sleep in a hammock and sometimes I snore.

2
4
5
6
8

I could play games all day
such as red light green light.

And when I'm tired I close
my eyes for the night.

I love myself and so should you.

Give yourself a hug and be pleasantly and comfortably you!

Author Bio:

Meet Kazia Alysse! Kazia was born in Fort Knox, Kentucky with family roots in Jamaica. She is mom to a happy and fun-loving 7-year-old named Kaden. Kaden was recently diagnosed with Autism also known as neurodivergent. Kazia has a passion to help others learn more about autism. With this book dedicated to Kaden, she would like to showcase the importance of self-love and self-acceptance. Encouraging others to embrace and enjoy their differences. Every child's distinctive story helps them reach their full potential and be their most confident self! Because in the end, everyone is beautiful and wonderful just as they are.